MODEL VETERAN AND VINTAGE CARS

By the same Author

PLASTIC MODEL CARS

THE HISTORY OF BRITISH DINKY TOYS 1934–1964

MODEL COMMERCIAL VEHICLES

MODEL
VETERAN
AND VINTAGE
CARS

Cecil Gibson

Consultant Editor—C. B. C. Lee

A Studio Book

The Viking Press · New York

Published in 1972 by THE VIKING PRESS, INC.
625 Madison Avenue, New York, N.Y. 10022

SBN 670–48251–X
Library of Congress catalog card number: 79–172070

Photography by Michael Langford

Printed and bound by C. Tinling & Co. Ltd.
Prescot and London, England

CONTENTS

Dedicated
to all my collector friends on the Continent,
especially Jacques Greilsamer
and Edoardo Massucci

INTRODUCTION

VETERAN CARS

Many of us began our collections with veteran car miniatures, perhaps because of all cars it is the veteran that is most attractive in small scale. It may be their old-fashioned appearance, the square bodies held high off the ground on thin-spoked wheels, their billowing cloth tops, or their multitude of shining brass fittings, but there is no doubt that these old cars are just as delightful in model form as the real thing. Vintage cars have much the same attraction, and their era is so recent that some can still be found in everday use. Many such models have been made, so that the whole story of motoring can now be shown in miniature.

A Frenchman, Joseph Cugnot, is credited with developing the first feasible road vehicle, a heavy three-wheeled tractor for pulling artillery. Luckily it did not work very well, as it must have been almost impossible to steer. The date was 1765, and the motive power was steam. The 19th century saw more experiments along the same lines; resembling heavy stage coaches with a steam boiler at one end, these devices were too uncontrollable to provide any competition for the railways, and it was much later, in 1885, that a new kind of engine was fitted to the first motor car. The internal combustion engine, driven by gasoline, had been developed by Karl Benz in Germany, and it is interesting that he seems to have intended it from the first as a passenger car, and that his design was so right that he continued to make the same car for the next fifteen years, by which time he had been overtaken by others, notably his fellow-countryman Gottlieb Daimler, and by the French.

In fact, quite a few people were making cars by the end of the century. In 1894 the first recorded motor race took place, and steam cars did well, their development having continued since the early disappointing experiments. They received a boost with the invention of the flash boiler, which gave a much lighter and more efficient power unit. Unfortunately, steam cars had to stop frequently to take on water and fuel, and the next race, the famous Paris-Bordeaux Race of 1895, saw gasoline-powered cars sweeping the board—possibly because the race was so long and the steamers had to stop so often for water (rather as if Jackie Stewart in one of today's Grand Prix races had to stop for fuel every 10 laps). The race was won by a Panhard, at an average speed of 15 mph for the 730 miles.

The Paris-Bordeaux Race turned most designers' thoughts firmly towards the internal combustion engine and away from steam, although steam cars continued to be made until much later, as were electric cars.

Those were the days of the 3 mph speed limit in England, requiring a man with a red flag to walk in front of all cars on the road. This out-dated and possibly dangerous law was repealed in 1896, and the first Emancipation Run to celebrate the occasion was organized. It is repeated annually to this day as the London-Brighton Run, which takes place in November. The first British car was the Knight, which appeared in 1895; American cars were running a few years earlier, and the Duryea is generally regarded as being the first of several cars in the States. Oddly enough, American development seems to have been independent of European ideas, and they were ten years behind, possibly because of the undeveloped nature of the country and the longer distances over which suitable roads were needed.

The Benz had an engine which produced less than 1 hp at 300 rpm and the whole machine was designed as a car. Daimler, on the other hand, conceived his gasoline engine as a power-pack for anything from boats to fire pumps, and the first Daimler was virtually a carriage with the horse taken away and an engine put in it. Later he saw his mistake, and he too designed what was to be typical of its day, a light four-wheeled car with the engine concealed at the back, running on high carriage wheels and steered with a tiller. By the turn of the century, cars like this could be found all over Europe and the United States, in comparatively small numbers but no longer rare sights, and still very much the preserve of the rich; from its earliest days the car has been one of the best and most exciting 'toys' a man could wish for.

After 1900, cars began to lose their 'carriage' look, partly because steering wheels took the place of tillers and partly because pneumatic tires on smaller wheels came into more general use, with equal-sized wheels front and back, which lowered the body and must have made steering more pleasant. If what might be called the Victorian age of motoring proved that cars could be made to run, the Edwardian era showed that they could be made to run more safely and certainly, and on occasions very quickly indeed.

EDWARDIAN CARS

The early Edwardian cars were the most delightful and charming, although in the years before World War I they began to acquire an over-bodied and over-stuffed look. They stood solidly on their artillery wheels and grey rubber tires, with a long hood running back to the cowl and, in front, a shining brass radiator of individual shape (many early cars could be recognized by their radiators, without looking at the badge). The driver was seated comfortably behind a rather vertical steering column with solid gear and brake levers at his side and a splendid rubber bulb handy, often attached to a long and serpentine brass horn. He could see all around without difficulty as he sat so high, and in any case had no windshield. Car bodies were beautifully made, hand crafted and painted. Their handsome lines were unmarred by anything except the one or two spare tires attached to the sides or the back, and perhaps a large trunk or wicker basket on the roof.

This era lasted from 1901 to 1914, a comparatively short period which saw tremendous development of the car as a more practical means of transport, and one which was no longer so expensive as to be available to very few. Chain drive gave way to shaft drive, more closed bodies were seen, and, perhaps most significant of all, light cars or 'voiturettes' became popular. The American Ford 'T' of 1908 was the first of the mass-produced cars that many people could afford. By 1914 there was a distinct division between the powerful and expensive prestige marques and the small light cheap cars for the man in the street. American monuments to the era included Winton, Packard, Mercer, Thomas, Knox, Stutz, Simplex, Oldsmobile, Pierce Arrow, Franklin, and Stanley.

THE VINTAGE ERA

World War I put a halt to mass-produced cars, but while the production of civilian vehicles ceased, aircraft-engine development brought many benefits, not the least of which was lightness. Light engines with aluminum pistons, overhead valves and abundant power were to transform the passenger car, and the war had also produced thousands of trained mechanics to service and maintain such a car. Four-wheel brakes, better chassis and steering, and electric lighting and starting transformed the car into something very like what we have today. The ten years after the war produced some of the best cars ever seen on the road, but perhaps craftsmanship and individuality were luxuries, too expensive for the motor car; by 1930 everybody who wanted a car could buy one, but it was not a particularly good one, even if it was cheap. Popular motoring had arrived, and design had stagnated in favor of cheap production methods. The vintage era was at an end.

We think of the big 3- and $4\frac{1}{2}$-litre Bentleys as being typical vintage cars, but in fact the Bentley is only one of the better-known of many sports cars (although vintage-Bentley owners allow of no others), and sports cars were a small proportion of the whole. The smaller Aston Martins, Bugattis and Frazer Nashes are possibly more representative of the type, and many family cars, such as Rovers, shared the qualities of good handling, light steering, and all-round quality found in the Bentley. Renaults in France, Fiat and Lancia in Italy, and in America the period Knights, Maxwells, Mathesons, Deusenbergs, Marmons, and others joined the endearing earlier makes that marked the 1920s; the best of these kept their vintage quality and keep it still.

It is fortunate that enthusiasts appreciated these cars and all they meant, and decided to restore and maintain them. The Veteran Car Club of Great Britain was formed in 1930 and the Vintage Sports Car Club in 1934, and there are many other similar clubs all over the world. It was decided that:

Veteran cars are those made not later than 1904.

Vintage cars are those made after 1919 and not later than 1930.

As this left a gap, *Edwardian* was the name given to cars made between 1905 and 1916, although these dates do not coincide with the reign of Edward VII, and to please people with fine cars made after 1930, the Vintage Sports Car Club recognized the category of 'post-vintage thoroughbreds'. In America, the dating is different, and an *Antique* is any car built more than twenty-five years ago, while a *Classic* is one built between 1925 and 1942 which, by reason of price, engineering or other criteria, is deemed distinctive. This means that the big 1935 Packards are Classics but not the 110 and 120 Packards of the same date. This may seem confusing, but in many ways is more sensible than the British system.

A NEW INTEREST IN OLD CARS

Immediately after World War II, many people were concerned with getting a new car, but it was not long before motor racing and rallying began on a limited scale, and soon the precious old veterans were being taken out of storage and made ready for the road. This took time, and it was some years before the old car movement got going. When they did, they found public interest greater than ever before. In those dull days (when most cars were painted in dark colors), the veterans, sparkling in their bright paint and brasswork, stood out wherever they appeared. In 1953, the film *Genevieve*, based on the London-Brighton Run, was tremendously popular, and by this time vintage sports car racing was well into its stride.

As always, toy cars reflected current interest. In 1949 at least two firms in America were making kits of veterans, mostly of balsa wood, cardboard and wire, but with the smaller pieces like steering wheels and lamps made out of plastic, and in 1953 the first of Gowland's 'Highway Pioneer' kits appeared. They were in 1/32 scale, were made entirely of plastic, and must have surpassed the manufacturer's fondest hopes.

11

Today these forty or so models are collectors' pieces, and it is rare to find a complete set. They did not sell so well in England, as in 1956 Airfix had started their series of veteran and vintage car kits in the same scale and very much cheaper; one of the first models was the Darracq from *Genevieve*. Even more important was the appearance of the first of the Matchbox 'Yesteryear' Series about the same time, and the combination of a thriving interest in old cars and the availability of bright, well-made and easily-stored models probably started more people collecting than anything else after the war.

VETERAN MODEL CARS

There is no record of the first toy car made, but it was probably a special model made for the son of some rich gentleman who had just bought his first Benz or Panhard. The best toys were made in Germany, where new methods of printing on tin had produced some splendid miniature boats and trains, and the German toy factories were soon turning out equally splendid cars, elaborately painted and often clockwork-driven. They were quite big, about 12–15 inches long, and often reasonably accurate copies of the real thing. Luckily, many of these toys have survived in the hands of specialist collectors. The French took over from the Germans after World War I, and in the 1920s firms like C.I.J. and JEP made some famous models, although probably the best-known of all were the promotional models made by Citroen, large tinplate toys of current Citroen cars and vans. These were so popular that at one time it was said that Citroens were losing money on their cars but getting it back on their models!

In those days the factories only made models of current cars, but up to 1930 and the official end of the vintage era, all such models were vintage anyway. This habit continued until the 1950s, when the revival of interest in old cars led manufacturers to make the first of many veteran models. These were no longer made in tinplate but in die-cast metal or in plastic, and were much smaller.

Die-casting was developed in the 1890s by the American firm that later would make the first die-cast toys, and still later would name them "Tootsietoys". A small limousine was made in 1911 and two model 'T' Fords in approximately 1/48 scale followed in 1914 and 1916. By the late 1920s the catalogues included a profusion of doll furniture, planes, trains, and games, and a wide range of automotive toys. The business of die-casting in lead had been taken up by several French manufacturers by 1930, and S.R., C.D., A.R. and Citroen made a number of models much sought after by collectors today. Tootsietoys reached their Zenith in 1933, when zamac was introduced to replace lead, and when the stylish Graham series came out, using concepts of design and assembly that were soon to be widely copied. In 1934, two European makers of toy trains began to produce model cars as 'O' gauge accessories. One was Märklin in Germany, and the other was Meccano, makers of Hornby trains, in Britain and France. The first six 'Modelled Miniatures' of the 'Hornby Series' were a prompt success and were soon renamed 'Dinky toys', a name happily still with us. Dinky Toys quickly came to pre-eminence amongst automotive miniatures, and by the late 1930s were supreme, while the quality of Tootsietoys had already begun to falter. After World War II, the high cost of labor and tooling put the Americans out of competitive contention, but Dinky Toys found new competitors at home, from Corgi and Lesney, and later from the makers of the beautiful collectors' pieces in France and Italy.

As America lost the price war in die-cast models, they became pioneers in the use of plastic as a modelling material. In 1949 they were offering kits with a few plastic parts, and in 1953 the Highway Pioneer series appeared. From that date a flood of ever-improving kits has come forth in America. The plastic moldings are beautifully clean and fit together easily, and construction is simple, so anybody can build a decent-looking model; there is endless scope for altering and improving each kit. The plastic is self-colored, although most enthusiasts paint their models, and chromed parts are provided—in the case of veterans, brass-plated parts instead. The popular scale is 1/24 or 1/25, with some series in 1/32, and many much larger models, up to 1/8. These large models are awkward to store, but give scope for detailing, and other countries are now producing them, for example, Pocher in Italy and several Japanese firms.

There are many types of mass-produced models people collect—tinplate, cast-iron, wood, rubber, slush-cast and poured metal, plaster, die-cast, plastic and even glass. There remains another type, the so-called scratch-built, in which the constructor makes every part himself. Some are fairly simple, but others are masterpieces of craftsmanship and take thousands of hours of work to complete. They are naturally very expensive, and are usually found in museums or in the hands of rich collectors.

MODEL CAR COLLECTING
This has only achieved the dignity of a recognized hobby in the last ten or fifteen years. Of course, many children do collect toys, and this may be the start of their interest, but people still smile at the thought of adults collecting small cars. An American friend of mine has a collection of 10,000 models, the value of which must be considerably more than

$24,000, and while this is an extreme case, it shows that the hobby is now fairly serious—and also a lot of fun.

There have always been collectors, preserving or perhaps finding again the models they bought as youngsters; enthusiasts for a particular car have tended to collect pictures, photographs and models of their favorite machines, so that members of the Aston Martin Owners' Club might keep models of Astons on their desks or in a small case to show how the car has developed over the years. And there are 'thematic' collectors (to borrow a word from philately), who are interested in fire engines, or buses, or Army vehicles, or racing cars, and build their collection around that one idea.

For a long time there was little contact between these individuals, but gradually the picture changed. In 1956 the International Association of Automotive Modelers was founded in America. At first this catered to scratch-builders, but now it deals more with super-detailing of kits and die-cast collecting. In the early 1960s a club was formed in France (replacing an earlier one) and in Italy, and these clubs bring out excellent magazines, with photographs of new issues and long articles covering early and obsolete models. In the United States COLLECTORS AUTO-MOTIVE REPLICA SOCIETY (C.A.R.S.) puts out an information quarterly newsletter, and a news publication, Antique Toy World, also has some interesting articles on model collecting. In England *Model Cars* has been in existence for many years, although it was only in 1965 that die-cast models began to be mentioned with any frequency. A dozen or more books have been published on the subject, usually about building models, but in 1966 *The History of British Dinky Toys* was the first book to deal with the products of a single factory, and in the following year the *Catalogue of Model Cars of the World* gave details of some 7,000 models, and provided an essential reference book, although this was not the first book on the subject.

There are now collectors' magazines in many countries, providing a meeting ground for the lone collector, although it is true to say that most of the pleasure in collecting comes from international correspondence and exchanging models through the mails, the only way of filling gaps in the collection when the models are no longer to be found in the shops. It may take years to find that one last model in a series, but the pleasure in finding it is all the more.

THE PLEASURES OF COLLECTING

Most people like collecting things, and with model cars the scope is enormous. There must be very few who simple buy every miniature car that comes their way, and most collectors develop a special interest. Some prefer tinplate models, some only die-cast. A collector of die-cast models may only look for those in the most common scale, which is 1/43, or in 1/86 (Matchbox size, roughly), or he may collect only French models, or the products of one factory (Dinky, Corgi, Mercury, etc.), or models of one make of car (Fiat, Ford, Ferrari), or on one theme (buses, tractors, racing cars). For some reason a die-cast model collector is seldom interested in plastic kits, but the kit collector has the extra pleasure of making the model before he puts it on display. Each country produces its own type; the Americans like early cast-iron toys and plastic kits; the French look for early tinplates and like to convert and repaint current die-cast toys; the Italians are particularly keen on hand-built models in large scales; the Japanese tend to collect dozens of models of a particular car; and Britons like early Dinky Toys above all else. Some collectors have even come to value old catalogues and historical material as much as the models, themselves.

It may seem that all this takes up a lot of time and needs a large amount of money, and it is true that for one or two people it has become a full-time occupation. But of course the beauty of the hobby is that the collection can be as large or as small as desired, can be taken up or left alone as needed, can be used to demonstrate either the history of the motor car itself or the development of the toy, and makes you many friends here and abroad. You must be interested in cars to begin with, and you are fortunate if this interest happens to be in veteran or vintage cars, as they make delightful models, colorful and bright. Luckily there are many firms making such models. In England, Matchbox make most of the veterans, Corgi make a few, Dinky practically none. In France, Minialuxe, Norev and Safir make good plastic toys, R.A.M.I. made metal veterans, and Solido make some of the best models available anywhere, a range of the big classics of the 1920s; in Germany, Ziss and Schuco; in Holland, Best Box; and in Spain, Eko are the names to look for. In Italy, Politoys make some good models, and Dugu and Rio make both veteran and vintage cars, probably the most beautiful available anywhere today. America still makes the best plastic kits, with such names as Aurora, Lindberg, AMT, MPC, Johan, Pyro, Renwal and Revell generally available throughout the world. The Japanese kits are almost as good, and they have recently started producing veterans, too, as do France and Italy. In Britain they have Airfix, whose moldings are excellent despite their low cost, and whose kits are often the bases for conversions.

This is not a full list, but it shows that the old-car enthusiast is well

15

catered for still. With rising prices, few people nowadays could afford to buy, restore, maintain and drive one veteran car, but a collection of miniatures provides, at little cost, a great deal of the pleasure and interest to be found in these machines, and the entire history of that long-departed, fascinating and tempestuous age of motoring can be spread out on the space of a table top.

THE MODELS

1 LESNEY YESTERYEAR MODELS

The Yesteryear models are responsible for awakening interest in many collectors. They are cheap but the castings are first-rate, the modelling accurate, and the paintwork good. First seen in 1955, the series is still continuing.

Top row: The 1926 TYPE 35 BUGATTI is the archetypal vintage race car. Note the neat louvres along the hood, the realistic treatment of the wheels, the external gear and brake levers (not quite accurate), and the genuine 'Bugatti blue' finish. The 1926 MORRIS COWLEY 'BULLNOSE' is also very vintage. The rear opens to show the rumble seat, and the radiator is brass. The 1908 GRAND PRIX MERCEDES—1908 was a classic year as far as racing cars were concerned, and, this big 12-litre Mercedes was typical. The large exhaust pipes, the chain drive and the spare tires mounted at the rear are also typical.

Second row: A later MERCEDES, THE 36/220 OF 1928, has longer, lower lines, external exhaust and a fold-flat windshield. The frontal view of the 1912 PACKARD LANDAULET shows the radiator shape and the high and ungainly styling of this era. The 1906 ROLLS ROYCE SILVER GHOST is a rather unfortunate color, but the long rivetted hood and the 'broken' windshield are typical.

Third row: I doubt if the original of this model FORD would have been painted anything but black, but the color here suits it. Like all these little cars, this would benefit from some touching up, for example, black for the springs and steering wheel, silver for the lamp glasses, etc.* The 1909 THOMAS FLYABOUT does not look genuine in a metallic finish, but the detail work is excellent. The 1910 BENZ LIMOUSINE is another tall car—gentlemen expected to be able to get into their seats without knocking off their top hats, and there should have been no difficulty in the Benz.

Bottom row: A 1911 RENAULT TWO-SEATER. The driver and passenger had an excellent view of the countryside around them. There is a spare tire by the driver's right hand—no wheel, just the tire. The fine spidery wheels of the yellow 1911 DAIMLER are effective, and the fluted radiator shell is nice. Daimlers always look good in this strong yellow color. The 1909 OPEL COUPE has had the top removed to balance the picture, but it looks better this way. The seat upholstery is well done.*

---

* Though beware! Some collectors feel strongly that any tampering with original finish, no matter how worn, badly degrades the value of a toy.

2 CONTINENTAL VETERANS

First seen in 1958, these little cars tend to be slightly larger than their British counterparts, are brightly painted with a profusion of brass parts, and are often spoiled by slightly clumsy wheels in dull plastic. The cars portrayed are usually French or some variety of Ford.

Top row: Who could fail to be captivated by this 1895 ROCHET-SCHNEIDER by R.A.M.I.? The driver sits at the back, has a tiller to steer with, and is sheltered from the sun by a parasol arrangement. The passengers, less fortunate, are in the full light of the sun. Its companion is a PANHARD LEVASSOR of the same year, and it, too, has tiller steering and much larger rear wheels. This model is made entirely of plastic, whereas the R.A.M.I. is made of die-cast metal.

Second row: Another all-plastic model is the Minialuxe 1907 FORD, which is more simply made but gets the lines well. The brass parts are vacuum-plated plastic, and look reasonably effective. The 1924 CITROEN by R.A.M.I. is a splendid little beast. (It is a vintage car and not a veteran.) Painted metal gives a much better finish than colored plastic, and the solid wheels look less offensive than spoked wheels in plastic.

Third row: The 1892 'TOIT BOIS' (WOODEN ROOF) PEUGEOT by Safir is made in metal, with the wooden roof simulated in plastic. The passenger sits in the front, but facing the driver, so in this case he does not see an accident approaching. The model on the right is a Safir 1910 RENAULT COUPE, and is a rather ugly little model of a rather ugly little car, very square and upright. The glass windows are good, and the model is peculiar in having a metal chassis and mudguards and a plastic body.

Fourth row: A German model this time, by Ziss, a 1908 OPEL STADTCOUPE. German firms started making veteran cars much later than anybody else, and they never seem to have caught up. This Opel is fairly simple, and is let down by the wheels, although the radiator casting is nice, with the maker's name in script across it, a common feature of the time. Ziss make German veterans only—and the inevitable Fords. Another Ford by R.A.M.I., a FORD MODEL T OF 1908. The body casting is good, but the radiator is something of a let-down. Driver and passenger do well under a large cloth top, but the 'mother-in-law seat' at the back is rather out in the cold.

3 ANCESTRAL MOTOR CARS

All but one of these cars were made in the nineteenth century, so they should look alike, but there is a vast difference between them, even in their outlines. This provides much of the interest on this page.

Top row: The first motor-car, the BENZ OF 1885. Made by Cursor as a promotional model for Mercedes Benz. The Benz is a beautiful example of accurate plastic molding. Even the engine flywheel at the rear of the model spins round, in a model just $2\frac{1}{2}$ inches long. The four-wheeled 1886 DAIMLER by its side is a similar promotional model by Wiking, another German firm which has made similar Volkswagens for VW dealers as well as a large number of smaller plastic models. This is a beautiful model, too, with slightly more detail than the Benz—the front axle swivels, and the engine and transmission are accurately reproduced. Such models are expensive and are a little fragile, but are dear to the collector's heart.

Second row: The 1896 4-HP PARIS-MARSEILLE PEUGEOT, looking rather unready for such a long journey. The makers, Safir, have made spoked wheels by scoring clear plastic discs. The center model is a R.A.M.I. PANHARD LEVASSOR TONNEAU OF 1895, steered by a long tiller. An attractively colored and surprisingly heavy little car in metal. The Minialuxe JAMIESON on the right is much simpler, in plastic, with opening engine covers at the rear. An interesting detail is the distance between the gear and brake levers, not, as is more usual, on a common mount. It uses the method of scoring clear plastic to represent spokes, too.

Third row: The 1878 LA MANCELLE AMEDEE BOLLEE is one of R.A.M.I.'s best models. An extraordinary-looking device, it had a large brass boiler mounted at the rear. The stoker had a canopy over his head surrounding the long chimney and he must have communicated in some way with the driver, proudly in front but some distance ahead of him. Between them, and decently concealed by a large canvas canopy, sat a couple of intrepid passengers.

Fourth row: Two R.A.M.I. models, on the left the 1898 HAUTIER ELECTRIC TAXI. This is virtually a hansom cab without the horse. The driver sat at the back and steered hopefully, looking over the top of the roof, and the passengers entered from the front. Charming and a bit ridiculous. The SCOTTE on the right is a steam car dating from 1892. The boiler is at the front, to the left of the driver. How pretty these cars looked with chimneys belching smoke and fringed tops fluttering!

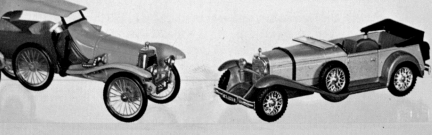

4 MOTOR SPORT IN MINIATURE

Many enthusiasts collect nothing but racing and sports cars, and the attraction is obvious, especially as car racing is so popular. The models here are all of machinery with a sporting character of some kind.

Top row: Two Renaults from the great days of inter-city races. That on the left is the metal Safir PARIS-VIENNA RACER OF 1902, and recaptures the stark and brutal lines of the original, which won the race. This is one of my own favorite models; note the radiators mounted along the sides of the hood and the high seats for driver and mechanic. I could not say how accurate is the color of the model on the right, a plastic replica of almost the same car by Minialuxe. This is the 1903 PARIS-MADRID car and is not nearly such an attractive model as the other.

Second row: Norev make their models exclusively in plastic, but the molding and coloring techniques are now so good that the body of this 1928 SSK MERCEDES is almost as good as painted metal, and the chroming is also very successful. Its companion is a 1912 SPA made by R.A.M.I. The boat-tailed body and long sweeping mudguards are very typical, as are the twin spares at the rear and the divided windshield. All the models in the R.A.M.I. range are based on actual originals in the Musée de Rochetaille, near Lyon in France.

Third row: A Czech firm, Igra, makes this 1906 LAURIN AND KLEMENT in several versions, this being the racer. It is a pretty if simple little model, but a success for a first try—the Czechs make a large number of models, but I think this was their first 1/43 scale veteran. The 1904 28-HP DAIMLER is not strictly a sports car, except that it was an adventure to drive any car in those days. But the lady and gentleman look as if they are setting out to enjoy themselves. The model is by a firm called D.C.M.T., which produced a now classical series of models in 1957 (including one of the *Genevieve* Darracq). The combination of metal body and plastic accessories is quite good, but the radiator and lights can do with some touching up with gold paint.

Fourth row: Before World War I it was common to buy a chassis and have a special body built to one's own design. This 1914 PANHARD ET LEVASSOR has a 'skiff' body made by the French firm of Labourdette. Behind the hood the bodywork is wooden, made in the way as a light boat or skiff would be made. The whole thing is strange to our eyes, but Minialuxe has made a good job of this model. The 1928 SS MERCEDES is by Solido.

5 BRITISH MANUFACTURERS

It did not take long for our local factories to realize that the special collectors' model was likely to prove popular, and in 1964 Corgi started their own Classics Series. We tend to look down on these comparatively cheap models, perhaps because they are seen more frequently than the costlier Continental models, but they are almost as good, and in some cases better, than their Italian or French counterparts.

Top row: The Corgi 1910 RENAULT 12/16 is a good example of this French make, and a neat little model. Brass accessories add to the effect. The BULL-NOSE MORRIS COWLEY (like the Bentley, an inevitable choice) is one of the few veteran models made by Spot-on, a firm now absorbed into the Dinky empire, but continuing under its own name in New Zealand. This is a neat reproduction of a famous car with the artillery wheels and the rumble seat of the 1920s.

Second row: The Corgi 1927 BENTLEY. Corgis are masters of the art of using up molds, and this Bentley was first issued some years previously in a couple of variations. The 1915 FORD MODEL T is in a fetching shade of pale blue, a color favored by restorers perhaps, but certainly not by Henry Ford. I like the poor man trying to get it going at the front.

Third row: The Corgi BENTLEY in its original guise, although red is not a happy choice of color. The brake drums show up well against the wheel spokes. Another Bentley, the BLOWER $4\frac{1}{2}$ by Spot-On. The color is far too light, the wheels are a bit weak, and the driver's scarf is blowing at right angles to his ear, but the fold-flat windshield and the Union flags on the sides make an appealing model. Funny how the super-charged $4\frac{1}{2}$, a car disliked by W. O. Bentley and not a real success, has stuck in the minds of enthusiasts and manufacturers alike.

Fourth row: Two Corgi models, the 1912 40/50 ROLLS ROYCE on the left must surely be one of the classic models of all time. The detail is perfect, the paintwork superb, the casting of the luggage rack unequalled, and the Silver Lady mascot never bettered. I only wish I could like it more. The 1910 DAIMLER, on the other hand, is a marvellous model, despite its bright orange finish. Normally I hate plastic figures on a model, but here they are beautifully finished and fit perfectly. A real classic.

6 GREAT NAMES IN MOTORING

Many of the famous makes of the early days of motoring have disappeared or been absorbed into large corporations. Half of the cars displayed on this page are no longer seen on the roads. All the models have right-hand drive except for the Mercedes, and all are collectors' pieces.

Top row: This 1914 LANCIA THETA by Dugu has been produced quite simply without a great deal of highly-chromed accessories, and is all the more effective for it. Most Lancias look good in small scale, or perhaps I just like Italian cars, but this model is much more realistic than, for instance, the Mercedes below. The R.A.M.I. 1908 PANHARD ET LEVASSOR VOITURE DE MAITRE is painted in rather garish colors. It was one of the earliest veterans offered by the French company, and seemed attractive when it first appeared in the shops, but it is crude by today's standards. The spare wheel is under the cover on the roof.

Second row: Dugu's 1912 ITALA is one of two versions, the other sporting an enormous white top. This one is painted a pleasant shade of red and has a second windshield for the rear passengers, and a large brass horn in the form of a serpent's mouth agape on the off-side front mudguard. The 1912 DAIMLER by the Spanish firm of Eko is in plastic, but nonetheless effective. The details are slightly crude, but with this material and the cheaper price, this is not surprising.

Third row: The 1919 HISPANO SUIZA by the same firm is a simple but good reproduction of this famous make, and is one of a series of veteran cars made in Spain by Eko. The body lines are interesting. The MERCEDES KETTENWAGEN by Ziss; this could only be a German model, a rather ugly car crudely reproduced. The paint is well done, although the maroon looks wrong with bright red wheels, and even the lamps look uncomfortable.

Fourth row: The Rio 24-HP FIAT is one of the many old Fiats made by Continental firms in the last ten years. I don't know that I like the colors much—there could not have been many red-roofed limousines even in 1905—but the lines are good. It is impossible to leave out RENAULT when discussing early motor cars, and this is a typical Renault shape. The model is interesting in that it reverses the usual order and has a plastic body with metal chassis; notice, too, the ear-trumpet by the chauffeur's head and the brass-plated accessories.

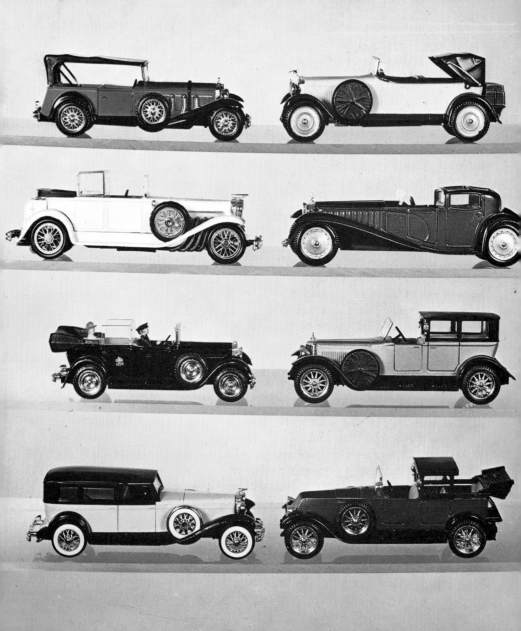

7 CLASSIC CARS–
CLASSIC MODELS

In the vintage era there were many famous cars—and some duds too; in the last ten years the better Continental toy manufacturers have produced some quite beautiful models. When the best of both worlds go together, as in the models here, the results are collectors' classics.

Top row: The 1928 MERCEDES SS is the closed version of the model in plate 4. (Most of these models can be obtained in either open or closed versions.) A small criticism is that the wheels are too brightly chromed. The 1926 HISPANO SUIZA H6B is beautifully painted in chocolate and cream with the flying stork emblem proudly on the radiator. The cloth covers on the spare wheels are well done, and the small wind wings at the sides of the windshield and the trunk at the rear are typical. The model is by Solido.

Second row: A Dugu DUESENBURG OF 1931—slightly outside our terms of reference as a vintage car, but allowable as an American Classic. Four large external exhaust pipes lead through the mudguards to the muffler. It is the double-cowled phaeton with rear-seat windshield. The Solido BUGATTI ROYALE depicts one of the rarest and most sought-after of all vintage cars. Only six Royales were made, and four were sold. This sedanca de ville was originally owned by Ettore Bugatti himself, and the sweeping lines of the fenders are particularly beautiful.

Third row: The rest of the models are all Solidos. This is the 1926 FIAT 525N owned by the Pope, who is in the back seat. Note that His Holiness's registration number is 1 SVC. A handsome 1925 8-CYLINDER PANHARD ET LEVASSOR, the photograph showing a somewhat angular line, although this is less marked in other views.

Fourth row: The DUESENBURG MODEL J. Like the Dugu on this page, this is a little out of its time, but there is no doubt of its importance in American automobile history. The pale blue color is very nice against the black fenders. The wheels are a little bright, but the whitewall tires are faithfully reproduced, and the chromed covers over the spare wheels are extremely good. This is a car from the same year as the white Duesenburg, but it looks more staid than its sporting sister. The 1926 RENAULT 40 CV was a large car and far too dignified to be called sporty. More a car for a warm afternoon in the country in fact.

8 COMMERCIAL VEHICLES

A whole book could be written about the many different types of delivery vans, buses, etc., and luckily manufacturers are alert to the appeal of such vehicles in veteran form. Another volume in this series is devoted to them.

Top row: Another of the promotional models by Cursor, this 1896 DAIMLER was made in Cannstatt. Not quite so pretty as the other Cursors, this has the simple lines of a cart, with the power pack stuck on the back. A nice touch on the model is a strip of velvet along the driver's seat. The bright yellow GAMA is a three-wheeled postal van of 1910; rather a simple casting too, with the Imperial eagle cast on the sides. There is no indication stamped on the model of its factory of origin.

Second row: A 1911 AUSTIN DELIVERY VAN by Minialuxe with heavy lines, although this is normal in such vans. Nice, solid-looking plastic and 'veteran' lettering. Another Minialuxe, the 1907–1910 RENAULT BREWER'S DRAY, is equally simple and not a particularly good model.

Third row: Two delightful buses. The one on the left is a Rio, and one of the best bus models available today. The 1915 FIAT 18BL BUS had a four-cylinder 5·6-litre engine which must have given this twenty-seater a useful performance. The ladder to the roof rack is a nice touch, and the model is perfect, from its square radiator to the little brass lamp at the rear. The sun curtains are drawn on the nearer side. The other bus, by Eko, is a 1912 HISPANO, with similar lines. This is a considerably cheaper and less complicated model. The entrance is at the rear, and the passengers sit facing each other on two long benches. Mail is carried.

Fourth row: A different medium, two Gowland & Gowland plastic kits from the 1950s. Left, the 1904 OLDSMOBILE LIGHT DELIVERY TRUCK, very much of its time with the handsome curved line of the roof and the oval side-windows. Steering is by tiller. This model has been painted plainly, but an extra effect can be obtained by copying or cutting out veteran-type advertisements and sticking them on the sides. The other van is a 1910 INTERNATIONAL HARVESTER. This company, which also, rather confusingly, made farm machinery, made passenger cars as well as vans like the one illustrated, which has simple lines, an open back and a buggy roof. Although made recently, this model is now quite rare. Some collectors prefer to collect kits as boxes with the parts in unmade condition, but this seems to be taking things a bit far, even for 'collectors' pieces'.

9 AIRFIX 1/32 SCALE KITS

There are two popular scales for plastic kits, 1/32 and 1/24, although recently there have been 1/12 and even 1/8 scale models. Airfix kits have always been cheap, but they are of good quality; the moldings are first-rate and the kits make up into very good models. Veteran cars form only a small part of the Airfix range but have attracted many newcomers to modelling. If a gross mistake is made it is no hardship to throw away the resulting mess and start again, and they are useful for people who want to build variants of standard models—the set of wheels alone is worth the money.

Top row: A 1902 DE DIETRICH. A chain-drive monster with large flaring front fenders and rear fenders extending over the chain, very typical of the period. This is a difficult model to make and paint neatly, as is its companion, the 1904 MERCEDES RACER. This does not look racy at all, being fairly vertical. The driver has a comfortable seat, the mechanic crouching by his side has a less comfortable perch, but, after all, he was expected to be busy during the race. A spare tire is mounted at the back.

Second row: A 1910 FORD, looking very Early American, although the pale blue color is not authentic. The 1950 ROLLS ROYCE DOUBLE PHAETON has never been very popular with collectors. Perhaps it does not look dignified, although it is a genuine enough copy of the real thing.

Third row: 'Genevieve' in all her glory. While veteran purists would shudder at the idea of calling a car by name, there is no doubt that 'Genevieve' has stuck to this 1904 DARRACQ. This model is in a slightly larger scale than the others, there are fewer pieces and they are stronger and less liable to snap in the hands of an inexperienced builder, so for this reason it is an excellent kit to start on. The dark green Ford is a 1912 MODEL T, with a 'mother-in-law's' seat at the rear. The top and its framework are pleasing.

Fourth row: A LANCHESTER 1907, somewhat odd-looking about the front. Lanchesters had their engines in the middle, and the driver sat at the side of, or in front of, the engine. A hinged lid could be raised to let the driver into his seat and then formed a protective cover over his knees. The car was steered by a tiller, and, like all individual cars, Lanchesters are highly prized by veteran-car collectors. The 1911 ROLLS ROYCE is a much more Rolls-like effort than the other on this page, with a long shining metal hood and high bodywork. This car always reminds me of a taxi. This molding, or one very like it, was popular with manufacturers, and Gowland and Merit both used it.

10 EUROPEAN PLASTIC KITS

All but one of these kits were manufactured in France or Italy. While American firms can count on millions of customers, the European market is comparatively small, and few kits are available. The cars tend to be local products and the kits expensive.

Top row: The outer two models are by the same maker, Europe Model Kits (E.M.K.) of France. The one on the left that resembles a wardrobe on wheels is the PANHARD ET LEVASSOR 1895 COUPÉ DE VILLE, and the black car on the right is another PANHARD OF 1891, a much nicer model. The center model is interesting; it is the 1914 REGAL from the Lil' Old Timers range made by Hudson Miniatures, and is the original 1/32 plastic kit. The plastic, incidentally, is not polystyrene, and normal cements cannot be used. Hudson Miniatures also made larger wooden kits in the late 1940s and four of these were copied in the smaller scale and the new material. The interesting point is that the molds were sold to Revell, who re-issued the models in Great Britain but not in America.

Second row: The LE FARDIER DE CUGNOT OF 1769 by Precisia, whose range of old cars is appealingly named 'les Teuf-Teuf'. This is a simple ladder frame with artillery wheels, and is an excellent model apart from the historical significance of the machine. The box under the driver's seat is a basket for logs.

Third row: E.M.K.'s 1905 TONNEAU ROI DES BELGES PANHARD is a difficult kit to make up neatly, but the result is worth the effort, an extremely handsome body with the family's luggage on the roof and an early example of a sun panel over the driver. The remaining models are by Aviomodelli, an Italian firm. The first is an ITALA in Targa Florio racing guise, the rear half of the body behind the seat pared down to a bare chassis with two spare tires. These models are easy to assemble.

Fourth row: A 1924 ISOTTA FRASCHINI (the same car as that in plate 5), which is said to be 1/30 scale: the Italian makers are possibly more decimal-minded than we are with our 1/24s and 1/32s. A simple model with comparatively few parts and suitable for a beginner, which the other models shown on this page are certainly not. Both Avio-modellis have been left in their natural plastic color, and only the seats and accessories have been painted—again a useful point for a beginner. Possibly the Isotta's mudguards and chassis could have been painted black, but the model looks well as it is. A coat of clear varnish may be used to give a more authentic shine to the bodywork.

11 GOWLAND'S HISTORICAL SERIES

The most important set of plastic kits ever issued, the original thirty models were designed by Gowland & Gowland and issued in America between 1953 and 1956, many of them available in Europe slightly later. The famous American firm of Revell later distributed these kits and the models were subsequently called Revells. The models were to a fixed scale of 1/32, although two extra double-sized (1/16) models were also produced; these are not so prized as the original Highway Pioneers.

Top row: The 1914 STUTZ BEARCAT, the two-seater Ferrari of its day. Note the drum-shaped gas tank behind the driver. The 1913 MERCEDES stands high on its solid wheels, a fast Continental tourer of the era. The big headlights have been turned back to front to keep the glass clean and the chain drive to the rear wheels has a metal cover.

Second row: A 1907 RENAULT, a model I think of as a taxi. The model captures the shape admirably, the famous hood falling away in front (the radiator itself lies behind, at the cowl, immediately in front of the driver). The 1910 PIERCE-ARROW has a high windshield and top and a long hood, a fine American touring car of the time.

Third row: The Hudson of the same date. Close examination will reveal that this is exactly the same model as the Pierce-Arrow, and here the manufacturer has been a bit crafty. The chassis is over-printed 'Hudson' underneath, and the top has been replaced by a folded top boot. By painting the models differently (different body colors, and brass instead of nickel parts) and by putting the models at different ends of my display cabinet I have managed to keep the secret. The 1912 PACKARD is one of the old 1951 Hudson molds reissued by Revell, and for such an old pioneering kit it compares favorably with recent models. There are no chrome-plated parts, but this does not matter.

Fourth row: The 1910 CADILLAC; a square no-nonsense body, although notice the decorative fillets by the driver's head and the curly speaking-tube by his ear. (Most of these kits came complete with plastic figures in the correct period costume to stick in the seat and hold the wheel, but I find these almost caricatures and do not mount them in my own models.) The 1904 RAMBLER should be, and is, a rather ugly car—the radiator shape is one of the least appealing—but its very clumsiness makes it rather nice. Perhaps it is the heavily buttoned leather seats.

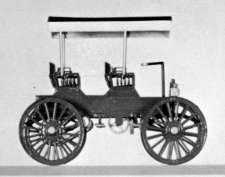

12 EARLY AND DELICATE

Veteran cars were never so beautiful as in the first ten years of this century, and some of the prettiest 1/32 plastic models made from kits are illustrated here.

Top row: One of the first Highway Pioneer kits, the 1907 SEARS BUGGY, is driven by a twin-cylinder engine under the driver's seat—part of the mechanism is clearly seen. A relic from the horse-and-buggy era is the fringed canopy.

Second row: Another Pioneer, the 1909 STANLEY STEAMER, has delicate lines, double cantilever springs and a complete lack of weather protection. The 1905 HUMBER with the high windshield was produced in small quantities by the British firm of Guiterman, which apparently only produced two models of five that were scheduled. The body is not particularly delicate, but it is included as a rare collector's item.

Third row: Revell's CURVED-DASH OLDSMOBILE with figures. When properly painted these figures lend interest and realism to the models, and certainly enhance the simple lines of the famous Olds of 1904. Steering is by tiller, and the engine lies at the back, started by the small brass handle on the driver's side. The center model is the other Guiterman kit, the 1905 VAUXHALL. This view does not show the clean modelling of the brake lever and horn, but shows the low-mounted external radiator and the fluted hood edges which Vauxhalls retained until very recently. The 1893 DURYEA is ten years older than the rest of the cars, and has obviously simpler lines. The wheels are positively spidery and the springs look fairly flexible. This early American automobile is beautifully reproduced in this kit, which has unfortunately now become very rare.

Fourth row: The 1903 MODEL A FORD has some fine brasswork in front of the driver, although I am not very sure what its purpose can be. There is no attempt at protecting the occupants from the weather and no doors in front at all—one simply stepped up and into the seat. The passengers entered such tonneaus from the rear. A charming touch is the provision of wicker baskets on either side, which must have made picnicking rather a pleasure. The 1900 PACKARD ROADSTER is a rather plain model, but the lines are very typical of the period—note the large brass oil lamps.

13 VINTAGE CARS

We have exceeded our age limit with some of the models here, but as the cars were at least designed in the late 1920s and are really vintage or classic in concept, they have been included. The American kits shown here have advanced to a more sophisticated level, the hoods come off to show a detailed engine, or the radiators and bumpers are chromed. They are all to the same scale, 1/32.

Top row: Pyro's 1932 LINCOLN K.B. DUAL-COWL PHAETON. One of a series of American Classics, this is an interesting car with a huge body. The passengers are completely separated from the front seats, and have their own windshield. The spare wheels in fender-wells, the vast bumpers, even the rear lights on stalks, are typical of the period.

Second row: Two Airfix kits, showing clever utilization of the same moldings for each model. The 1923 TWO-SEATER and the 1926 TOURER look quite different, purely because of their shapes from the windshield back. Both have neat artillery wheels.

Third row: Three great sports cars from Pyro. Left, the 1931 ASTON MARTIN. This model is based on an actual car, and the number plate—HX 4323—shows that this is an ex-works team car, LM 7, a two-seater built for Le Mans (where it was remarkably unsuccessful) and other races. The details are extremely well done, the hood lifts off, and even the windshield wipers are portrayed. The black Bentley is a 1930 SPEED SIX, a change from the inevitable blown $4\frac{1}{2}$ and has the correct tapered radiator shape. It has been painted to show a fabric-bodied tourer, and is a good model of this heavy-looking machine. It is a nice change to paint the model black, as Bentleys are usually green. The 1931 ALFA ROMEO is a companion to the Aston, and gets the lines of this Italian car to perfection. From the neatly-molded radiator to the gas-tank caps and the spare in the tail, this is a 1930 racing car at its best.

Fourth row: Another Pyro classic American car, the 1930 PACKARD SPORTS COUPE. The sombre black paint is probably not a good choice, and the bodywork with the slightly clumsy roof-line not very interesting, but the Packard bird on the radiator indicates that a great chassis and the famous Packard straight-eight engine could live down almost anything the coachwork specialists could dream up.

14 LARGER VETERANS

An assortment of these popular kits with one outsider in the shape of a metal Rolls Royce.

Key

	1	2	
3		4	5
6		7	8

1. Graphic Designers' 1907 SILVER GHOST ROLLS ROYCE, made in a soft metal alloy and extremely heavy. This 1/25 scale kit was made in Britain about 1955, and was screwed rather than glued together. It was expensive and did not survive the competition of contemporary plastic kits, so is now quite rare. It is so heavy that the chassis eventually bows slightly under the weight of the body.

2. Hudson Miniatures' 1910 INTERNATIONAL HARVESTER.

3. Hudson Miniatures' 1911 MERCER RACEABOUT, a handsome model and the early version in wood of the same car in plastic immediately below it (No. 6).

4. Aurora's 1914 STUTZ BEARCAT, another car to the 'raceabout' formula of a large slow-revving engine on a sketchy two-seater chassis. What fun they must have had in America in those days, especially when trying to stop these heavy powerful cars with somewhat inadequate brakes.

5. Fador Smallster's 1908 BAKER ELECTRIC Fador was another firm that brought out a series of wooden and cardboard veteran car kits, impressed no doubt by the early success of the Hudsons. Apart from a different box there is no way of telling these two makes apart.

6. Aurora's 1913 MERCER RACEABOUT. A most impressive sight with its mass of gleaming nickel-plated parts. The body is big enough to allow special painting effects such as the white lining here, done in this case with a mapping pen and Indian ink, although other methods can be used. Note the small collapsible seat for a third passenger on the left.

7. Aurora's 1911 BUICK BUG. The hood lifts off to reveal a twin opposed cylinder engine.

8. Hudson Miniatures' 1911 BUICK, the same car but modelled in wood. A simpler but still delightful model.

15 CAST-IRON MODELS

There are several types of models we have not shown in these pages of illustrations. One is the special one-off model built by a professional model-builder to individual order, and this has been excluded because there are so few about. Similarly, the old toy of the 1890s or the early 1900s is now found only rarely and then in specialist collections, and we have tried to illustrate this book with toys and kits which are comparatively recent and can still be found, or with actual current models. There remains a large and important section of cast-iron models, mostly American and quite simply made. Some were molded in one piece, others were cast-iron two-piece molds simply screwed or rivetted together, and making a crude but extremely strong toy. Quite a few of these survive, due to their indestructibility and are to be found in many collections.

The color plates show a selection of makes. Most of them are so simple that it is impossible to put a name to the car portrayed, although one model has 'AUSTIN' cast on the sides. These 1920 toys can still be found in America, although, except for Hubley, the names—Arcade, Champion, Kenton, Kilgore, Dent and the like—are strange to European ears. The models shown are all small; the better examples are bigger, and some are very handsome indeed, having many parts, and often a shiny nickel-plated driver.

16 COLLECTORS' PIECES

Up to the early 1960s model cars were virtually the same as they had been for the previous thirty years, simple die-castings with moderately good paint, no real attempt to depict interiors, seat, dashboards or steering wheels, and no effort to show the different textures that make up a real car. The metal body, the canvas top, and the chromed grille were all painted die-castings. Corgi had put windows in their 1950 models and other British manufacturers followed suit, but the results were simple and a little crude. Features like spring suspension were introduced in the late 1950s, as were opening hoods and doors—the hoods being more popular at first, revealing a rather shiny engine. At the same time, friction drive for 1/43 scale models was discontinued, presumably because it was unpopular; all these features were introduced as sales gimmicks, and Corgi in particular has always been in the forefront in producing this sort of novelty, which appeals greatly to children. Admittedly, the 'Christmas-tree effect' is displeasing—a model with too many features, opening and badly-fitting doors and hoods, highly-chromed metal parts where no chrome should be, etc., loses the basic lines of the car. But a good model absorbs its special features, and is still a pleasure to see.

It was a brave decision in 1960 to make expensive models for collectors, but the two Italian firms, Rio and Dugu, who started the idea, have been amply repaid. The products of these companies, and later Solido in France brought a new dimension to collecting. I remember seeing the first of these models in Monte Carlo and being surprised at the quality of the Dugu Fiat (illustrated). The thing was obviously so much better than anything seen before; unfortunately the price was so much higher, too, and in America duty brings the price of many of these little cars to over $6·00 each.

What makes these models so different? They are obviously made to be kept and cherished, and the very boxes are different. Each model is based on an actual car, the present trend being towards taking a particular car from a museum or a private collection and making an accurate repro-duction, down to the number plates. Many Dugu originals can be seen in the Carlo Biscaretti di Ruffia Museum in Turin, and the Museum sells a special series of Dugu models—the 'Museo' series—lower priced than the average Dugu, and slightly simpler in make-up. The Museum is one of the most beautiful and interesting in the world, and is well worth a visit, even a special visit to Italy, to see its collection of cars and motoring miscellania.

Specialist miniatures do not concentrate much on opening doors, etc., although some have this feature, and Solido models usually have opening doors and hoods, and spring suspension. The first thing one notices is the overall beauty and accuracy of the model. The body is very cleanly cast in metal with doors and hinges, rivets and louvres clearly delineated. The paintwork is good and proper vintage colors are used. Lining is put in neatly. Many of these models cleverly combine metal and plastic, the chassis, fender and running boards being made of dense shiny plastic which simulates metal very well. The interiors are complete with realistic buttoned upholstery with the right amount of shine, a steering wheel, gear lever and brake, and windows and screen where appropriate. The touring top, whether erect or folded, is again the correct texture (dull black or white canvas usually), and may be tied down or braced with real leather straps.

The small parts of the model are equally well done; the radiator is a plastic molding with a dull black grille inset and chromed or brass plated as appropriate, the badge or name clearly visible. Headlights have crystal 'glass' inserts, and horns with serpentine brass convolutions lead from the rubber bulb by the driver's hand to the front fender. The wheels are molded for the individual model—not just a standard disc—the rear wheels may have the correct extra number of spokes and the tires are of rubber, white-walled if need be, and with the correct tread. The model is just as interesting from below, as springs, engine, sump and transmission are all depicted.

It is difficult to know which of the large range of models available to choose from, but the models illustrated here are Rio and Dugu veterans (with the addition of a couple of 1924 Isotta Fraschinis).

Top row: The 1894 DE DION BOUTON STEAM VICTORIA, a large, stately and comfortable-looking model. The front half is a straight-forward steam car, the rear half is pure horse-and-buggy. One can almost imagine the old Queen sitting in this in the grounds of Balmoral, minus a pony and John Brown. A pair of oil lamps is mounted on the front of the Victoria portion, and a nice touch is the accurate modelling of the wheels—each of the three pairs of wheels is different.

Second row: The model that caught my eye in Monte Carlo, Dugu's first classic, the 1911 MODEL 4 FIAT. The photograph catches the grace and dignity of the car's heavy body, and the realistic contours of the canvas top, braced in this case with leather straps. The other car is the FIAT 24-HP DOUBLE PHAETON OF 1906, another large car of over 7 litres' capacity. The driver sits in a sort of double sedan chair, his contact with the world restricted to honking that splendid horn at passers-by, while the owner and friends enjoy the sunshine in the back seat. The high rolled-down roof at the back is very typical.

Third row: Two ISOTTA FRASCHINIS from some fifteen years later, already showing modern lines, and a considerable departure from veteran days. The 1924 TIPO 8A SPYDER on the left is the sporting version with vast chromed headlights, a large open body with twin spares mounted at the rear, and a small roof over the passengers, who cannot have had much protection. The bumpers, the upright split windshield, and the spotlight by the driver are all in period. Like the other cars on this page, the driver's place was on the right, where the manufacturers of those days felt he should be (in fact it is not until comparatively recently that Lancias started to make cars with left-hand drive). The other car is from the same year, and is the same chassis with closed bodywork. The lines are pleasant, and, although hardly modern, would occasion no great surprise if seen on the road today. Driver and passengers are separated, the chauffeur in this case has a cloth canopy over his head. (Another model from Rio is identical but has the canopy rolled back.) The spare wheels in this case are carried on each side of the body, and the chromed radiator is well done.

Fourth row: The Dugu 1909 35/45 ITALA is a stately carriage, with nickel-plated accessories setting off the dark green body to perfection. Its companion is a 1909 BIANCHI LANDAULET, another tall and delightful vehicle which is quite a masterpiece of Baroque wirework. The elegant rack on the roof is the equivalent of today's trunk, and could take a surprising amount of luggage. The chauffeur has a half-glazed windshield in front of him. The engine of this car was a four-cylinder 5-litre unit, which produced 25 hp at 1250 rpm.

The color plates show a fair cross-section of the motor car in miniature and explain some of the fascination of model-car collecting as a hobby. They also show the development of motor-car design over some fifty years. Veteran cars, with their mass of intricate detail, make particularly good models, and are some collectors' first and only love. Many others are interested only in racing cars or commercial vehicles (two subjects which will be covered in other books in the Troy Series), or the products of a single factory.

With some 10,000 model cars to pick from, some limitation of the field is obviously necessary, and most collectors quickly find and develop their particular theme. Current interest in the preservation and driving of old vehicles has undoubtedly brought many people into the hobby. As it happens, some of the best models ever made have been of veteran or vintage cars. I hope this book has shown why they are firm favorites with so many collectors.

GUIDE TO THE MODELS

The following models are shown in the color plates; the following notes on country of origin, material and scale are given for those who may find some of the names unfamiliar.

AIRFIX (GB) 1/32 plastic kit
AURORA (USA) 1/16 plastic kit
AVIOMODELLI (Italy) 1/30 plastic kit
CORGI (GB) 1/43 die-cast
CURSOR (Germany) 1/40 plastic
D.C.M.T. (GB) 1/43 die-cast
DUGU (Italy) 1/43 die-cast
EKO (Spain) 1/43 plastic
E.M.K. (Europe Model Kits) (France) 1/32 plastic kit
FADOR (USA) 1/16 balsa wood, card and wire kit
GAMA (Germany) 1/43 die cast
GOWLAND & GOWLAND (USA) 1/32 plastic kit
GRAPHIC DESIGNERS (GB) 1/25 metal alloy kit
GUITERMAN (GB) 1/43 plastic kit
HUDSON MINIATURES (USA) 1/16 balsa wood, card and wire kit, also
    Lil' Old Timers series 1/32 plastic kit
IGRA (Czechoslovakia) 1/32 plastic
LESNEY YESTERYEAR various scales die-cast
LIL' OLD TIMERS *see* Hudson Miniatures
MINIALUXE (France) 1/43 plastic
NOREV (France) 1/43 platic
PRECISIA (France) 1/32 plastic kit
PYRO (USA) 1/32 plastic kit
R.A.M.I. (France) 1/43 die-cast
REVELL (USA) 1/25 plastic kit
RIO (Italy) 1/43 die-cast
SAFIR (France) 1/43 plastic
SOLIDO (France) 1/43 die-cast
SPOT-ON (GB) 1/43 die-cast
WIKING (Germany) 1/40 plastic
ZISS (Germany) 1/43 die-cast

INDEX